Sexual Abuse Survivors
and the Complex of Traditional Healing

(G)local Prospects in the Aftermath of an African War

Mats Utas

NORDISKA AFRIKAINSTITUTET, UPPSALA 2009

NAI Policy Dialogue is a series of short reports on policy relevant issues concerning Africa today. Aimed at professionals working within aid agencies, ministries of foreign affairs, NGOs and media, these reports aim to inform the public debate and to generate input in the sphere of policymaking. The writers are researchers and scholars engaged in African issues from several disciplinary points of departure. Most have an institutional connection to the Nordic Africa Institute or its research networks.

To ensure the actuality and relevance of the topics in these reports, the Nordic Africa Institute welcomes inputs and suggestions from readers in general and policymakers in particular. Please e-mail your comments to: birgitta.hellmark-lindgren@nai.uu.se.

Indexing terms:
Civil war
Sexual abuse
Women
Victims
Humanitarian assistance
Traditional medicine
Healing
Post-conflict reconstruction
Reconciliation
Sierra Leone

Language checking: Wendy Davies
Photos: Mats Utas

ISSN 1654-6709
ISBN 978-91-7106-648-0

Contents

Introduction

In *Young female fighters in African wars* (NAI Policy Dialogue No. 3) our intention was to give a broad overview of the ways in which young women actively endured African independence and civil wars. We furthermore wanted to draw attention to the situation for young women in the aftermath of these wars. In *Sexual exploitation and abuse by peacekeeping operations in contemporary Africa* (NAI Policy Notes 2009/2) we approached the problem of sexual exploitation and abuse in peacekeeping missions on a continental basis. In this study the purpose is to give more specific insights into *sexual abuse and local healing methods* from the aftermath of one war: the Sierra Leone civil war (1991–2002). Although the focus is on a specific country, it is not my intention to limit the audience to humanitarian aid workers and policy makers interested in this country only, but rather, by giving enough depth to a single case study, to open up a more general discussion on the question of *whether and how traditional healing methods can, or should, be included in postwar aid programmes.*

The United Nations and many international non-government organizations (INGOs) involved with emergency aid in African conflicts have for some time been debating this issue; whilst at the same time very little scholarly literature have been available to throw light on it.[1] This text takes a hands-on approach to these questions by digging into the complexities of local socio-culture and tradition while at the same time giving some very specific suggestions on how practically to proceed in the field.

Sierra Leone is in the process of recovering from a long, protracted internal war that ravaged large parts of the country between 1991 and 2002.[2] During the war children were both used directly as weapons of war (Robertshaw 2004) and targeted as victims. In the process, girls and young women were particularly exposed, being victims of targeted sexual abuse

---

1. Noteworthy exceptions include the works of Alcinda Honwana (1997, 1999, 2001) and Carolyn Nordstrom (1997a, b) and, outside Africa, of Alex Argenti-Pillen (2003). See also the research review by Susanne Kaplan (2005).
2. For a historical overview see Gberie (2005), Keen (2005), Richards (1996)

and abduction. It is for instance estimated that approximately 50,000 to 64,000 Internally Displaced Persons (IDPs) may have suffered war-related sexual assaults (Physicians for Human Rights 2002). Even if the figures are considerably lower in the post-war society we note that sexual abuse is still frequently reported. For example, in Kenema District 97 cases of sexual abuse were reported during the first six months of 2004 alone.

Local society and culture offers a vast pool of tools and resources that can be used by external actors in order to make development and emergency projects efficient. However cultural resources are often ignored and at times even shunned. After a civil war, for instance, preference is given to creating new "Western" institutions to help local communities develop or return to balance instead of using existing locally tuned institutions. The creation of trauma centers and skills training programmes are a case in point when it comes to aiding young survivors of sexual abuse during and in the aftermath of civil wars. As many social structures crumbled during the civil war there is an urgent need of immediate assistance to young people who have suffered from sexual abuse. It may be true that in the short term the most efficient way (in terms of time and money) is to bring in well-established healing methods from the outside. However, there will be an urgent need to "localize" such healing methods in order to have a long-term positive outcome in a country like Sierra Leone – that is, of healing being sustainable once the emergency aid effects have decreased.

The aim of this policy report is thus to locate social paths and structures which cater for psycho-social healing that have local legitimacy and are therefore able to work efficiently in the mindsets of peoples in the local arena. To this end, I discuss in this study a *Sierra Leone traditional healing complex* that comprises a number of overlapping actors, or "departments" as one actor proposed calling it, namely herbalists, Soweh mammies (heads of the female secret societies, also written "Sowei" or "Zoe"), Mori-men (Muslim healers/diviners), Karamokos (Muslim teachers), and Christian pastors. There are three interrelated forms of healing that must take place after a young person has been sexually abused, namely: medical, psychological and social. Direct medical healing is mainly catered for by herbalists, psychological healing by the Karamoko/Mori-men, and social healing by churches and Soweh mammies and in the ancestor bush. They all have their specific roles to play as will be further outlined in this study.

6

2. Scope of the study

The aim of this study is threefold. Firstly, the study takes a detailed look at sexually abused girls' and young women's life situations. What is their status in the post-war setting? How are they coping with their traumatic experiences? Who is aiding them in their efforts? Secondly, the study aims to locate and describe traditional healing practices that cater to young people who have been sexually abused. Thirdly, it seeks to make recommendations to agencies concerned with the reintegration and psycho-social wellbeing of young Africans in war and post-war settings.

The primary aim of this study is to locate and describe the various local and traditional healing practices that respond to children and young people who have had traumatic experiences in relation to sexual abuse during and after the Sierra Leonean civil war. When addressing local or traditional trauma practices, a broad definition of tradition is used, including instances of trauma healing within the religious practices of Christianity and Islam. The initial assumption that the interaction between Christian, Islamic, pre-Arabic, and pre-European healing practices has been prevalent is confirmed in this study. The main task of the study is to discuss healing by the Sierra Leonean traditional healing complex. The study will also provide a picture of how survivors of sexual abuse are living in the various communities and how they are socially and culturally perceived by the community. Such matters form the basis of a deeper understanding of how traditional healing methods work in the various communities. The research will guide the reader into the various healing practices that are available to young people who have been sexually abused and provide particular recommendations for people and agencies who wish to work in closer cooperation with local and traditional healers in the field. As the aim of the research is to point to new directions it should be observed that this is a pilot study into a field enmeshed in secrecy, both in relation to the sensitive cases of young people who have experienced sexual violence and also to the profound secrecy among some individual healers of secret and other types of societies. As such the study sheds light on issues of trauma healing but also calls for more research to be carried out in the field.

2.1. Methods

The study is based on fieldwork conducted for 16 days (July 29-August 13, 2004) in four districts of Sierra Leone. The districts targeted in this study are: Western Area, Bombali, Kono and Kenema Districts. The aforementioned geographical targeting includes both urban centers and rural areas. The target for the study was to interview 30 young people (both girls/young women and boys/young men) who experienced sexual abuse during the war and 30 young people (both girls/young women and boys/young men) who experienced sexual abuse after the war. The study also focused on conducting an unspecified number of interviews with chiefs, leaders and traditional healers. In this effort, three different questionnaires were designed in order to target the different groups of research subjects. The questionnaires were designed so as to allow open-ended answers in an effort to obtain broad-based responses from the interviewees. Due to the sensitivity of the questions asked, and as the researcher is a male European, two young Sierra Leonean women were hired to carry out the interviews with the female participants. In cases where the research subjects had limited knowledge in Sierra Leonean Krio and the research assistants had limited knowledge in the local language spoken by the interviewee, local translators were used. Local translators were most frequently used in the interviews with older people. In total 50 young female survivors of sexual abuse between the ages of 12 and 41 were interviewed in the four districts. Even if below the original target, for reasons discussed below, the researcher believes that the sample group is large enough for important conclusions to be drawn. The study includes an additional 42 interviews with community leaders and traditional healers, further unraveling a fascinating social complex of traditional healing methods.

2.2. Research ethics

Researching sexual abuse is without doubt a sensitive field. The researcher and research assistants did their utmost to proceed carefully in order not to put survivors of sexual abuse at any risk of, for example, stigmatization, and resurfacing of emotions that threaten to intensify individual traumas. In this effort the research team worked through UNICEF implementing partners with individuals who were already involved in community outreach projects for child sexual abuse survivors. The questionnaires were checked by local social workers to identify and avoid sensitive questions. Furthermore, counsellors and social workers who were acquainted with the survivor and in turn who the survivor trusted were asked to be present during interviews to ensure as non-threatening an environment as possible.[1] Wherever possible, locations that were secluded and private were used for conducting the interviews. During data collection no names were recorded (either of survivors or healing practitioners) and in order to maintain anonymity people quoted in the text are only referred to by category of person, town/district, and age in the case of survivors. Pictures used do not contain images of people, and citations have been re-worded in order to maintain the confidentiality of the interviewees. The objective of interviewing 30 young survivors of sexual abuse after the war was withdrawn by the researchers due to ethical considerations. The various implementing partners of UNICEF had worked with post-war cases only to a limited extent. The possibility arose of interviewing more recent survivors of sexual abuse (one police officer offered to share all names and addresses of recent cases of sexual abuse with the researchers), but without a counsellor familiar with the survivors' case the exercise would have been ethically questionable. The interviews with the five post-war survivors were conducted together with the young girls' counsellors.

---

1. This did not work perfectly in all locations but overall was quite satisfactory as we did not encounter any mishaps during the work.

3. Limitations of the study

It is self-evident that, regardless of the background, conducting research on the subject of sexual abuse by interviewing the survivors is a very challenging task. How to approach such a delicate area and deciding what the qualitative outcome of a one-off encounter with a survivor of severe sexual abuse amounts to are both questions that need to be posed and looked further into. The truthfulness of the information disseminated during the interviews needs to be questioned and then the value of the results has to be taken into account. This study is not able to entirely bridge the gap between narrated story and reality; however, the use of female Sierra Leonean research assistants contributed to a narrower reading of the stories of the survivors. This dilemma between fabrication and truth has to be kept in mind when one encounters survivors' stories that are extreme similar to those of others in civil wars.[1] Yet there is sometimes a natural urge for survivors to tell anyone the truth in its entirety. Another factor that limits the willingness to provide correct accounts is the high number of researchers who pass through, ask the same questions and simply vanish. This became apparent during the field study in a rural area of Bombali District where a total fatigue in relation to trauma programmes by NGOs was expressed. During the field visit the research team was unable to meet certain young survivors of sexual abuse, as they did not appear for scheduled interviews, even though they had been previously notified and had already consented (on arrival the research team were told that the young women were on holiday or had left for the farm). Similar non-consent was encountered in two more villages in Bombali District. Continued research could have been a way of abusing both local communities and individual survivors in an area where over-interviewing has fatigued the survivors. Therefore, it is recommended that NGOs take

---

1. I have elsewhere used the term *victimcy* to discuss the practice of fabricating personal histories of extreme victimhood in contacts with international NGOs as *victims*; *victimcy* being the practice of presenting oneself as a victim (Utas 2005a, b). As Peter Metcalf has noted in his book *They lie, we lie* on ethnographic truth, "it is swimming against the intellectual tide to discuss the truth that ethnographies may contain" (Metcalf 2002: 1). In this context we need to be aware of layers of "truth" and different versions that are told, depending on audience and setting.

account of such reactions in communities and reflect on whether continued research or programme activities might in fact do more harm than good. This notion of fatigue was also observed in Makeni:

> *I don't need any help from anybody, especially not the NGOs. They come and interview us times without number. They promise to open skill training centers, giving us money to start petty trading, but at the end of the day we don't get anything from them. So I am tired of getting interviewed.* (17-year-old girl from Makeni)

Certainly such sentiments will limit findings. UNICEF staff based in Makeni were very aware of these problems and concurred that with lots of empty talk and no factual support this is a natural outcome – echoing a common saying among local NGO workers referring to the multitude of sensitization workshops they themselves participate in as "just another talk-shop".

Another problem is that projects based on external ideas are likely to make participants of these projects prone to comply with the dominant discourse. In this case the dominant discourse is the lingo of the NGOs, urban space and Christian churches, a somewhat adapted version of early-day missionaries. Up to the present day, the UN, INGOs and to some extent urban NGOs show skepticism if not outright contempt towards "traditional society". Centrism around urban modernity has further cemented this; however, for some reason urbanites, from the study sample, seem to be more at ease talking about traditional healing than many of the people in the rural areas. Among the young women in this study there are certainly efforts to look more urban. The stigma of being *munku* (backward) and having a preconception of how the NGOs want them to be tend to guide the interviewees' responses to questions asked during interviews.

Research might therefore have obtained more honest answers from young survivors of sexual abuse who had not already been interviewed in other NGO projects. However, this would have meant a much more time-consuming process in order to locate the interviewees and would have been ethically problematic with regard to both social exposure and the risk of re-awakening the experience of trauma within the individual survivor.

Recent anthropological literature on Sierra Leone has been dealing with the issue of secrecy (see for example Shaw 2000, 2001, 2002; Ferme 2001; and, for elsewhere in the sub region, Bellman 1984). Secrecy is especially pronounced when it comes to ritual societies such as Poro and Bundu (the main male and female secret societies),[1] and is also very much part of all the traditional healing practices that are dealt with in this study. During an interview with a Soweh mammy (ritual leader in the Bundu Society) in Makeni the research team was initially able to receive an unprecedented amount of information; however, it became apparent shortly after that contradictory statements were uttered from one sentence to the next – eloquently done in order to cover up previous statements. The notion of secrecy became evident, which added further challenges when research was undertaken. This secrecy was encountered a number of times and was expressed during an interview about psychological healing with a chief's wife in Kono District:

> *The Digba (alternative term for Soweh mammy) will take me to the secret bush and perform a ritual. And that I will not expose.* (Chief's wife in Kono District)

To approach such secrecy is a difficult task; however, not all healing takes place inside the Bundu bush and Soweh mammies are also allowed to share some knowledge with outsiders on how to cure those who have suffered sexual abuse.[2] The extent of their information is unknown, though. A symbolic death penalty faces anyone talking about these issues to the uninitiated, which further limits the number of people willing to discuss them. Other traditional healers also speak with a tone of secrecy, though appear to be more open to talking. Other more secular concerns might also inhibit people from discussing their practices. A traditional healer might be afraid of talking about treating cases of sexual abuse because they are supposed to go to the police first and because their clients often go to them clandestinely. A thriving Mori-man (Muslim healer/diviner) in Kenema, for instance, denied that he was treating cases of sexual abuse; however, his denials were contradicted by others who maintained that the healer was especially experienced in women's cases, and certainly had treated cases of sexual abuse.

Another problem with the study was that in several cases the implementing NGOs do not currently work with the young girls. For that reason the survivors were less willing to talk and the interviews were more schematic

---

1. There exists a rich literature on secret societies in the region (see Utas 2003: 92ff).
2. In her dissertation *Multiple meanings of female initiation* Liselott Dellenborg has an interesting discussion on secrecy and women (2007: 247ff) as well as secrecy in relation to INGO work (ibid. 226ff).

than those held with girls who were actively involved in current projects. In some cases NGOs were not able to organize the number of interviewees that were originally planned for. Closed skill-training centers, school holidays and the fact that the study coincided with a labor-intensive period on the farms (the replanting of wet rice) further made the endeavor problematic. In total 50 qualitative interviews where held and recorded. Despite efforts to do so, it was not possible to organize interviews with sexually abused young men. The stigma of being a sexually abused man seems worse than that of being a sexually abused woman, thus making male survivors unwilling to be interviewed.

Regardless of the shortcomings of the study, a solid overview was compiled of the various traditional techniques used when dealing with sexually abused young women.

4. War-related sexual abuse

In the first part of this section, an overview of a quantitative study regarding war-related sexual violence is presented. The comprehensive size of this study makes it suitable to draw statistical conclusions. The study draws on qualitative material as well as a deeper understanding of the socio-cultural powers at play in the Sierra Leonean case. The second part of this section is an overview of war-related violence based on the qualitative findings. The final part of this section discusses sexual abuse in post-war Sierra Leone. Has the war in the midst of all the brutality been able to change people's viewpoints on sexual violence and, and if so, could it actually lead to better formal and informal treatment of survivors of sexual abuse?

4.1. Quantitative findings

To gain an insight into the extent of the problem of sexual abuse during the Sierra Leonean civil war, it is worth reading the report by Physicians for Human Rights, *War-related Sexual Violence in Sierra Leone* (2002). With a focus on IDPs the team interviewed 991 household representatives about their families, thereby reporting on the experiences of 9,166 people. In the above report 8% of females and 0.1% of males were stated to have experienced war-related sexual violence. Most survivors reported being abused by the Revolutionary United Front (RUF) or the more diffused rebel groups. Forty per cent of the sample group recounted that they had experienced sexual abuse that lasted for more than one week. Only two thirds of those who had experienced sexual abuse stated that they had reported the abuse to another person – in contrast to this study where all interviewees were helped by someone after the sexual abuse. The reasons for not telling anyone were mainly shame, social stigma, and fear of being rejected by family and local community. In the Physicians for Human Rights report, only 40% (50 people who said they were seeking help after the assault) said they were helped by traditional healers, while 50% stated they had gone to hospitals. In this study a striking 83% of the sample group stated that they were initially treated with traditional medicine (but not necessarily by traditional healers) and only 12% by Western medicine. In the Physicians for Human Rights report 32% of the abused women stated that traditional healers had been the most important people in aiding them to cope mentally with the incident of sexual abuse. This quantitative data exemplifies the importance of extending knowledge in the sphere of traditional methods of trauma healing.

4.2. Qualitative findings

The voices of young women themselves can reveal the terrible ordeals they faced during the war years. As previously stated in the ethical concerns, all interview findings have been presented in such a manner as to conceal the identities of the interviewees. The following is a sample of statements by girls and young women about the sexual abuse experienced.[1]

> *I was abducted by a rebel called XXX. He was a commander in RUF and he took me to be his wife. I suffered a lot in his hands. He asked other rebels to tie me on a stick; to flog me. I was forced to have sex with him and his boys. I stayed with them for five years and I was trained and fought alongside them.* (21-year-old woman from Koidu)

> *I was abducted by the rebels from this village. They tied my feet to a big tree and a soldier put a gun close to my mouth and threatened to kill me if I shouted. He did it to me on several occasions till I got pregnant. He took me as his wife and brought me to Lunsar. He would force me to have sex with him any time he needed me. I stayed with these rebels for three years, they trained me as a soldier and I fought for them.* (20-year-old woman, in Bombali District, abducted when she was 13)

> *I was abducted by the rebels. They tied my feet when they wanted to abuse me. And they also abused me with a stick.* (20-year-old woman in Kenema District)

> *By then I was carrying my child on my back. He (the rebel soldier) took the child and sent her inside a blazing fire. He flogged me and then he raped me right in the middle of town. I was 18 at the time. My husband took care of me after he returned from the bush where he was hiding.* (27-year-old woman in Kono District)

Most young survivors of sexual abuse have also witnessed others being sexually abused. At times the mental scars of seeing others, particularly

---

1. Chris Coulter's study *Being a bush wife: women's lives through war and peace in Northern Sierra Leone* (2006, especially chapter 8) gives a well-tuned contextualization of the findings below. See also Mariam Persson (2005).

family members, being abused or even being forced to abuse other people, as in this case, might be as hard to cope with as direct sexual violence. This is expressed by a young woman in the following:

> *I saw my sisters being raped, I saw my father killed after first being forced to rape my elder sister. I have been witnessing lots of rape cases in the jungle. I was captured by a Captain who treated me really bad from the beginning – I have been raped by him, yet I am still living with him.* (19-year-old woman from Freetown).

This case also highlights structural dilemmas of dependency and uncertainty, even in the aftermath of the war, where a large number of young women are still living with the soldier who had abducted them. Naturally, some establish bonds of affection:

> *They tied my mouth so as not to shout, they tied my hands behind my back and had my legs tied wide open. Then he (the fighter) raped me.... Later the same people who raped me treated my wounds. Well I have been raped twice during the war and I have been witnessing how they raped a girl and an old woman. Later a Sergeant picked me as wife. He had plenty women and was beating me. Even now I am living with this man – I like him.* (21-year-old woman, who was twelve at the time of first being raped, Freetown)

We must also observe that some young girls were not only held for the direct benefit of the rebel soldiers but could also be used as junior wives. This young girl was only eight years old when she was abducted, and after being raped she became a servant to the wife of a rebel commander:

> *I was abducted by a rebel commander. He raped me in a nearby bush close to our village. He then took me along with him. His wife later on took me as her slave. She flogged me every day and she also starved me, because she said I was her husband's junior wife. I was eight years old when they held me.* (16-year-old girl in Kono District)

Two more girls included in the original sample group were held as junior wives, but were not interviewed as they stated that they had not been sexually abused during their time as abductees.

Another cause of great aggravation to many young survivors of sexual violence is that they know the perpetrators well and that they are sometimes still living within the same community. The aggressor might even hold an official position in post-war society. Despite the common knowledge of the abusers' past crimes, there is little chance to prosecute them or even get child benefit:

I know the abuser very well. He lives at the xxx-barracks and is working in the army. It is really frustrating for me going through these experiences when I know that the perpetrator is alive and not punished for the crime he committed. And further he is not assisting me with anything for the child I got from him. I sometimes want to go mad . (19-year-old woman in Makeni)

Even if the abuser is dead or no longer in the same community the traumatic experiences of sexual abuse during the war are frequently re-experienced by the survivors in the form of nightmares. Many state that they try to keep themselves busy in order not to think too much about their traumatic experiences. As described below, a number of the techniques used by traditional healers are aimed at erasing the survivors' memory of abuse.

I can dream of what happened. In my sleep I can start to shout. My mother will then come and talk to me. We will pray over it to forget. Still, at times I want to go off (feel I am going mad) because when I was with them I used to take drugs, like cocaine, but now I am not in the habit of taking them. (17-year-old girl in Kono village)

The young woman who had witnessed her father rape her sister stated:

I still do not believe it – that my father was forced to have sex with his own daughter just to be killed afterwards. I cannot leave this thinking behind: he was crying "Please, please my daughter forgive me, before he died". Up to this day I can recall his voice several times a day. (19-year-old woman in Freetown)

Many of the young survivors still re-live their experiences in dreams and thoughts even if treated with the medicines of Mori-men, herbalists or the prayers of imams and pastors. In some cases they will try alternative "medicine" – like the young converts in this study who left the Mori-men and Islam behind to search for remedies in the Christian church.

There are a few accounts of boys and young men being raped by rebel soldiers. In some places they state that "rebel women" raped young boys, but talking about rape of men by men seems taboo. People state that the low incidence of this is due to homosexuality being rare in Sierra Leone, but it can also indicate that the stigma may be too extreme to even mention.

Yes, because the rebels force them to have sex with their sister or mother. But I did not see rebels rape men, only women. (Soweh mammy, Freetown)

17

Recorded are several accounts where a male family member has been forced to have sex with a female family member (as in the example above). Yet no cases of male-male rape were identified through the interviews.

How are cases of war-related sexual abuse treated within the families, among friends and in the larger communities? To what extent have young sexually abused girls been accepted, and when have they been shunned? There is no one answer to these questions, but it seems as if the prevalence of sexual violence during the war made it somewhat easier to be the survivor of sexual violence. Many survivors of sexual abuse did talk openly about it.

> *Girls who escaped from rebels during the war would say it. They would not be afraid to say it to anyone. During the war people would talk about rape. When someone escaped to a different village people would say that it was because she had been raped.* (Pastor in Freetown)

Yet many survivors had experiences of mischievous and further traumatizing gossip and rumors. Young survivors of sexual abuse often state they were treated worse than what local community leaders admit to. Survivors recount how they were mocked by friends and people in the community, as in the cases of these three young women:

> *Sometimes when I pass in the street of our area some of my friends and neighbours will keep looking at me and say to one another, "Don't mind that girl, she has got rebel blood."* (19-year-old woman in Makeni)

> *At times even my friends mock me, calling me Mrs. XXX – the name of the rebel who abducted me.* (21-year-old woman in Koidu)

> *I got a child for the rebel. So people sometimes call him rebel pikin (child).* (20-year-old woman in Koidu)

Many families are trying to avoid the social stigma of having a family member who had been abducted or sexually abused by suppressing the matter. Many young women state that it is not something you talk about: *"We keep it as a deep family secret"*, as a 17-year-old girl in Makeni put it. A Freetown Karamoko (Muslim teacher) points out that many young people do not live in the homes of their biological parents but with foster parents, and according to him, *"if living with the extended family the sexually abused is often badly treated*". A 27-year-old woman in Koidu says that she has broken contact with her family altogether after they had put all the blame on her:

> *I spoke to family members about my experiences. They put all the blame on me saying I was disobedient to them, and that I was not home when the rebels attacked the village. So I stopped going around them because they never tried to encourage me.* (27-year-old woman in Koidu)

The feeling of social stigma makes it harder for the individual to get over the sexual abuse:

> *I suffered through this alone, without any punishment for the abuser, because family members were afraid of the scandal for our family. … My mother told me not to talk about it because if I do I will bring shame to the family and people will laugh at me and it will be difficult for me to get married.* (20-year-old woman in Makeni)

Even though these women are talking about the problem of burying their experiences among the family secrets, it is to some extent reassuring that in most cases women have not been cut off from their families, but live with them. The survivors are not thrown out most of the time, even if numerous "rebel women" dare not return to their home towns and villages, but still flock to urban centers. Yet, how does it look if we focus on marriage? Even in this field we have very disparate answers. Some people in the communities say that married women who have experienced forced sexual violence will be reaccepted when they return home and that young abused women will have no further problems, yet others say that there are a number of problems. Rather than defining a schematic overview, individual differences need to be addressed; however, the girls and young women are often more negative about their own future prospects than the people in their surroundings.

> *I am unable to get a husband because the rapist made me pregnant. For that reason it is difficult for me to get a man.* (20-year-old woman from Makeni)

Even some elders are negative about the survivors' prospects:

> *When the husband will learn about it, he will often divorce her.* (Soweh mammy in Freetown)

From a Christian perspective it is often stated that the young women who have experienced sexual abuse will have no problem getting married. Several pastors of Born-Again churches stated that they had church members who had been "rebel women" who had now accepted the gospel. Being "born again" led to their acceptance in the church and quite possibly also their re-acceptance into the local communities. This point may be reinforced by the incidence of conversion from Islam to Christianity (8-16%) among interviewees.

In the post-war setting female ex-combatants and girlfriends of combatants were commonly perceived as deviant and socially dangerous and it was felt that these ideas made reintegration difficult. Survivors of sexual abuse were treated no differently, as local communities in this study stated that they experienced problems with the return of young women from the rebel sides. There is both a mutual and gradual process of reintegration into society as pointed out by this teacher:

> *From the beginning we experienced a lot of problems with these girls but now they are cooling down.* (Teacher in Kono District)

If young victimized women feel stigmatized who are they then able to talk with? Many state that it is older female family members, such as an aunt or a grandmother, who they initially talk to and who help them through the early stages. Some will then open avenues of healing discourse within families and yet others will talk to friends as the accounts below point out:

> *I will talk to my grandmother about it, but not my friends as they would provoke me.* (21-year-old woman in Freetown)

> *I felt it was necessary for me to speak about it to my family members and also to friends. Because they all knew I was victimized. They always gave me words of courage and encourage me to put the past behind me.* (20-year-old woman in Bombali village)

> *We do not talk about rape openly but we will talk about it to each other – the others who have been raped.* (21-year-old woman in Freetown)

> *I only talk about it to one of my friends who is also a victim of sexual abuse and we give ourselves words of courage.* (20-year-old woman in Makeni)

There is no single way of describing how young girls are treated in the local communities and who they feel safe to talk to. Rather, this section has been concerned with showing the complexity of the problem and thus points to the importance of dealing with cases on an individual rather than a general basis.

4.3. Turning a page? Sexual abuse in post-war reality

I was on my way to fetch water for my mother when a man stood in front of his house and called me to go and buy bread for him. I went to him and he pushed me inside his house. He put cloth inside my mouth and then raped me. The abuser is our neighbour. At night I don't want to eat or talk to anybody. My mother will cry and say that if I go off (go mad) I will bring shame on her. (12-year-old girl in Kenema)

I was at the stream washing my clothes when three boys came and asked me to assist them. As I was going there they started to flog me and dragged me to the bush. There they abused me one after the other. (16-year-old girl in Kenema)

It is not good to talk to anybody about it. I don't want to spoil the good image of my family. (14-year-old girl in Kenema)

Some people go around and say that I am a grown-up woman because I am doing the same thing as they do. Others have told their children not to come around me. (13-year-old girl in Kenema)

Ninety-seven cases of rape were reported in Kenema District during the first half of 2004. The four accounts highlighted above are all from that period of time and are part of the effort to include post-war cases in this study. It is interesting to note that they all received emergency treatment in the hospital, that there are no herbalists or Mori-men active on their cases, and they received intensive counselling at the GBV (gender based violence) center. Yet, one is left wondering about the number of cases not reported to the police, or not admitted to hospital, and thus likely not referred to a GBV center. In interviews with traditional healers, it was evident that they still treat cases of sexual abuse, but are afraid to talk about it because of legal issues involved. In Makeni a Mori-man stated that the last case he had was six months earlier.

(When did you treat your last case of sexual abuse?)

Six months back – "I don mend am"[1] (Mori-man, Makeni)

From within the NGOs, workers state that the post-war sensitization on sexual abuse has been important and the police force's Child Protection Unit (CPU) also indicate the same. Imams in mosques are sensitizing people about AIDS. The number of sexual abuse incidences has decreased. Yet there is an obvious risk that the relative openness concerning sexual abuse during the war years and of the immediate post-war might experience a reversal. A Soweh mammy from Freetown proposes:

> *Today, after the war, we see it less frequently because people do not talk about it openly.* (Soweh mammy, Freetown)

This is but an indication, yet the case below, from Kenema, shows that even if a case is reported to the police the outcome can still be in line with how cases were solved prior to the war:

> *Sometime I can grow frustrated over the issue because the perpetrator's family came to my father and begged him, and my father agreed. So now the perpetrator goes unpunished.* (13-year-old girl in Kenema)

The following case in Makeni was committed during the war but followed a more ordered reality of Sierra Leone in peacetime as the abuser was, at the time, not a soldier/rebel:

> *After I was abused, my father sent some boys to the abuser to beat him up. A woman carried me on her back to the hospital and my father took the man to the police. The man was in prison for two days. Then he came to my dad with money to beg for forgiveness. My father asked him to marry me because he had spoiled me. Since that day he promised that he would come and do something in that way. But he pulled out and left the community.* (17-year-old girl in Makeni, sexually abused when she was 12)

The problem of extra-legality also features in people's ideas of the handling of sexual abuse cases, as in the account of this Karamoko:

---

1. "I have fixed it".

If people have respect for you in the community – even if you are guilty – the people will not let you appear in court, and as for the person, he will not go to jail. (Karamoko in Freetown)

In the efforts to locate psycho-social functions within the civil society (if we use the broad concept of the term and include institutions of the traditional sphere as well), discussions slide into both legal and clinical discourses a number of times. There is still, in the sensitized post-war period, a tendency to confuse the psychological trauma with hands-on themes such as legal settlement. For instance, many Muslim clerics in urban environments stress the legal aspects of Islam rather than the psychosocial healing of Karamokos' and Mori-men's ritual activities (see below). "Advice" is given to both abuser and abused and the aim is to settle the matter according to Muslim law. In Makeni one imam points out that Islam is a "guiding instance" but that if the parties can settle the matter – if for instance the abuser "puts kola" (asks for permission to marry – including dowry) – for the survivor it is a legal solution to the matter. Cases of sexual abuse and secret relationships resulting in an unwanted pregnancy are responded to with similar settlements and there appears to be a blurred distinction between rape and "woman damage" (pregnancy or lost virginity). A Mori-man in Makeni says that a Muslim family will often accept marriage as a compromise, as the girl "has already been tampered with".

> *It is a big sin, but if the perpetrator, or his parents, bring money and kola nuts (signaling that they are prepared to take responsibility for the girl/woman) and the girls' parents agree then they will let love intervene.*[1] (Mori-man in Makeni)

Another imam, who also practices psychosocial healing, while stressing the legal matter first, argues that such settlements are backward:

> *Big people, if not the police, will generally interfere in such cases. It is rare that the families will agree on marriage. It happens, but that is the native side.* (Imam in Koidu)

The prevalence of a clinical outlook is normal throughout the social spectrum. Rape cases in a normal setting are categorized as rape, and can only be clinically confirmed if a woman gets pregnant, loses her virginity (which is still often concealed by the family) or contracts an sexually transmit-

---

1. "Love" in this respect refers solely to the legal and economic aspects of marriage.

ted disease (STD). Local herbalists heal STDs with herbs and a Makeni herbalist talks of a medicine that can remake a woman into a virgin. Soweh mammies, as well, prefer to talk about the medical outcomes of rape: *"Some have stomach ache, gonorrhea and infections"*; only if pushed do they mention the psychological effects: *"At times some victims behave as if they are going mad"* (Soweh mammy in Bombali village). Surprisingly, there seems to be a greater emphasis on remaking the body into its "original" form than in talking about the psychological trauma of the survivor, which may be due to the perception of mental illness (see below).

To sum up on sexual abuse in the post-war era: it is less of a problem than during the war years, but still a significant issue. A rough estimate of the general incidence of sexual abuse can be calculated by using the statistics presented above with reference to Kenema District. These work out at approximately 200 reported cases of rape in 2004 in Kenema District. If we take this estimated figure and multiply it by 12 for the 12 districts of Sierra Leone then there would be 2,400 cases of sexual abuse in 2004 alone. (although Freetown in fact has a higher prevalence).[1] Yet only a small percentage of cases is actually reported. There is a risk, despite all the sensitization efforts, that sexual abuse will again return into the hidden parts of society. This might be even more pronounced as many of the people involved in the healing of sexual abuse are working in secrecy. On the other hand, the fact that they do work in secrecy also implies that survivors of sexual abuse can be treated without fearing the stigma that results from public knowledge, when hospital treatment and police investigations take place.

Despite sensitization there is still a long way to go when it comes to banning domestic violence and rape within marriage in Sierra Leone. Almost all of the young women in the survey, as spokespersons for a young generation of Sierra Leoneans, thought that it was the husbands' right to beat their wives, as the following two women (one urban and one rural) express:

> *Because he is the provider and he is stronger. If he does not love you he does not beat you.* (19-year-old woman in Freetown)

---

1. During 2004, 404 cases were reported to the Sexual Assault Referral Centre of the International Red Cross in Freetown during the months January-August.

It is right for a man to beat his wife if she disobeys him. (21-year-old woman in Kono District)

It is also commonly understood that rape within marriage does not exist as a married man has the right to have sex with his wife whenever he wants.

5. Variations of traditional healing

In this section, the issues highlighted relate to the spiritual world that most Sierra Leoneans share, the relationship between spirits and mental illness, and how this is linked with the traditional treatment of sexual abuse. In the second part, the various healing functions at work in Sierra Leonean society and an effort to unravel some of the cultural complexity found will be discussed.

5.1. Notes on mental illness in Sierra Leone

Most of them go crazy. They will be shouting out "come and rape me" or "stop these pains"; sometimes they will run around naked. (Karamoko in Freetown)

Some will lie down in the street with open legs and ask men to come and use them. (Soweh mammy in Freetown)

Running around naked in the street and abusive sexual behavior are two types of behaviour that Sierra Leoneans would commonly identify as signs of mental illness. The cause of such an illness would in the eyes of the different traditional healers, including herbalists, Karamokos, Mori-men and Christian pastors,[1] be evil spirits, called *djina* (or *jinn*), bush devils or demons, according to the particular religious belief. To give one example, somewhat related to cases of sexual abuse (and probably at times confused with it), is a common belief that dreams involving sexual intercourse – sometimes called "night husbands" for women – are the result of possession by an evil spirit. Dreams of having sex with a man, often a brother or a father, is commonly believed to make women infertile and also to cause spontaneous miscarriages. For young sexual abuse survivors the "night husband" category and the real life situation of sexual abuse are often con-

---

1. These four categories of healers are part of what I have called the Sierra Leonean healing complex that is discussed in detail below.

often conflated as they re-live experiences of sexual abuse in their dreams.[1] All women in this study who have heard about "night husbands" believe that they are caused by a bad spirit and cured by exorcism, a practice carried out by all the traditional healers interviewed in this study. The approach to curing someone of an evil spirit in cases of sexual abuse is very similar in traditional healing ceremonies to that taken towards "night husbands" as well as other "mental problems". Other researchers have noted that "illness and insanity … are located not 'inside' but rather are described in terms of invasion from the bush" (Shaw 2000:30). If mental illness is perceived as "outside" the body, in the guise of bush devils and evil spirits, this stands in harsh opposition to the Western psychological notion of individual inner mental states. It immediately appears as an obstacle to Western psychology in the Sierra Leone setting, thus calling for adaptations.

5.2. The healing complex

We do some of the same work as the "deep" doctors or the native doctors. Sometimes the Bundu Society will come to get small lasmami from the Alpha (Mori-man).[2] (Imam in Koidu)

It is the imam who treats people who are mentally ill and sometimes the "native people" in the [secret] societies. (Pastor in Kono District)

The Sierra Leone traditional healing complex comprises herbalists, Soweh mammies, Mori-men, Karamokos, and Christian pastors. "It is like we belong to different departments", a Mori-man stated to clarify how the various traditional healers differed from each other. In the following section the original intention was to maintain the different "departments"; however, in the course of the research, it became increasingly clear that the walls of the departments were easily penetrated and that most healers created their own

---

1. A Freetownian herbalist talks about how some of her customers mix up the two categories, yet she maintains that it takes different types of medicine to cure them. A pastor also points out that some clients have come to him to get healed from 'night husbands' but have later agreed that they have been raped. A 'night husband' might be the legitimate reason for getting aid for sexual abuse that is just too painful and shameful to talk about.
2. *Lasmami* is holy water produced by washing the ink off suras written on paper or leaves. The water and ink are put in a container and used to wash people in.

specific ritual confines superseding the departmental fields. Even if healing practitioners and practices have entered Sierra Leone at very different times, it is, as noted above, remarkable how consistent the various practices are with a more general cosmology. Rosalind Shaw has shown in a striking way how Muslim methods of divination and healing were reshaped, as well as, adapted to local forms of divination:

> ... skills of divination and healing do not form an untouched "traditional" baseline on top of which other forms of knowledge have been sedimented: they have been constituted and reconstituted in different historical contexts that have themselves become embedded within diviners' knowledge and experience. (Shaw 2002:104)

The arrival of Islam, the slave trade, colonialism and Christian missions are all historical forces that constitute and reconstitute the socio-cultural character of Sierra Leone. Furthermore, the latest historical forces, the civil war and the massive entry of INGOs onto the scene are part of this process, which includes reforming the healing complex, and being modified by it. If one wants to have an impact on the healing complex it is important not only to take an active part in the reform efforts but also to allowing one's own tools to be modified in relation to local complexities. During the study it became increasingly clear how the different healers made use of each others' methods, not only by appropriating them but also by recommending each others' knowledge to clients and/or buying certain types of medicine from each other. For instance the Mori-man would go to the herbalist and get certain herbs and the Soweh mammy would go both to the Mori-man for *lasmami* (holy water) and the pastor for prayers. This is the complexity that the clients engage in when dealing with traditional healing.

6. Traditional healing of sexual abuse

This section will first provide an overview of the various healing methods that the young women themselves say they have been using. For this task, a table covering all the interviews conducted with girls and young women who have been sexually abused is presented. This will give an overview which can be returned to in the other parts of this section. The first sub-section will also make some general comments on healing and cleansing rituals in relation to sexual abuse. In the second sub-section, the work of the (male) herbalist will be discussed. The third subsection will look at the work of Karamokos and Mori-men, and the fourth that of Soweh mammies and female herbalists. The fifth sub-section will outline cleansing ceremonies both inside and outside the Bundu bush. In the sixth sub-section we will move on to the churches and the healing work of the pastors. Finally, in the seventh sub-section, we will take a brief look at how Western forms of counselling are perceived, and raise a few critical concerns of how to relate western conceptions of self and sickness to the ideals of the traditional healing complex.

6.1. From the girls' and young women's perspective

The following table will provide a brief overview of the interviewees. Age, age at time of first sexual abuse, and length of time held, mainly serve as background information, while religion, initial treatment, psychological treatment and preferred treatment guide towards the methods used by young survivors of sexual abuse. Of immediate interest is, as mentioned above, that 83% of the interviewees who were sexually abused during the war state that they were initially treated with traditional medicine. Many of them did not receive the treatment from a herbalist but from relatives or other elderly people. It is quite apparent that good knowledge of healing herbs is common in these areas. It is also important to make the distinction between direct medical treatment and psychological healing. Secondly, no clear correlation between Muslim girls and young women and consultation of Muslim Karamokos and Mori-men can be established. Thirdly, eight women in the sample state that they are Muslim, yet see the church as the

Table 1.

Interview	Current age	Age at time of first sexual abuse	Length of time held/ abduction period	Religion	Initial treatment – who and how	Other psychological treatment	Preferred treatment
WA¹1	18	12	6 years	Muslim	Herbalist/trad. med.	Country doctor for treatment of "devil"	Counsellor
WA 2	20	14	3 years	Muslim	Family member/trad. med.	Prayer by imam	Prayer
WA 3	21	12	1 year	Muslim	Old woman/trad. med.	Counsellor	Counsellor
WA 4	21	11/12	3 years	Muslim	No treatment	Counsellor	Counsellor
WA 5	16	10	3 years	Christian	Mori-man/trad. med.	Mori-man	Mori-man, Karamoko
WA 6	19	13	Still with the man	Muslim	Mori-man	Mori-man	Mori-man, Karamoko Soweh
WA 7	11	n/a	n/a	n/a	n/a	n/a	n/a
WA 8	9	n/a	n/a	n/a	n/a	n/a	n/a
Ma²1	18	15 (?)	1 day	Muslim	Grandmother/trad. med.	n/a	Church
Ma 2	17	n/a	Not held	Christian	Trad. med.	Counsellor	Church
Ma 3	17	12	Not held	Christian	Nurse/Western	n/a	Church
Ma 4	20	15	Not held	Muslim	Trad. med.	n/a	Church
Ma 5	17	13	Not held	Christian	Herbalist/trad. med.	n/a	Counsellor
Ma 6	19	16 (?)	2 years	Muslim	Mother/trad. med.	Counsellor	Counsellor
Ma 7	17	12	n/a	Christian	Hospital	no	Counsellor
Ma 8	18	8	3 years	n/a	n/a	Church	Counsellor and Church
BD³1	20	13	3 years	Christian	TBA/Trad. med.	Church	Counsellor
Ko⁴1	21	17	5 years	Muslim	Herbalist/Trad. med.	Karamoko, Mori-man, Diba	Church
Ko 2	20	12	7 years	Christian	Family/Trad. med.	no	Church
Ko 3	27	17	6 years	Christian	Herbalist/Trad. med.	Mori-man, native doctor	Counsellor
Ko 4	27	16	1 month	Muslim	Mori-man/Trad. med.	Church, Karamoko	Karamoko Mori-man
KD⁵1	25	13	3 months	n/a	Mother/Trad. med.	No	Church
KD 2	21	14	n/a	Christian	Sister/Trad. med.	No	Church
KD 3	28	18	Not held	Muslim	Diba/Trad. med.	No	Church
KD 4	28	18	Not held	Christian	Nurse/Western	No	Church, converted
KD 5	28	18	3 years	Muslim	Elderly woman/Trad. med.	No	Native doctor
KD 6	17	10 (approx)	4 years	Christian	Hospital/Western	No	Church

					Herbalist/ Trad. med.	Mori-man, Karamoko	Counsellor
KD7	35	21 (?)	1½ year	Muslim	Herbalist/Trad. med.	Mori-man, Karamoko	Counsellor
KD8	41	37	Not held	Muslim	Dispenser/Western	Do not talk about it any more	Church, converted
KD9	16	8	4 years	Christian	No treatment	Bundu Society	Church
KD10	17	n/a	6 months	Muslim	Hospital/Western	No other	Church, Counsellor
KD11	18	9	10 years	Christian	Herbalist	Herbalist for trauma	Church
KD12	20	9	1 year	Muslim	Elderly woman/trad. med.	No	Church
Ke¹ 1, post-war	12	12	Not held	Muslim	Hospital	GBV Center	Counsellor
Ke 2, post-war	13	12	Not held	Muslim	Hospital	GBV Center	Counsellor
Ke 3, post-war	13	13	Not held	Christian	Hospital	GBV Center	Church, Counsellor
Ke 4, post-war	16	16	Not held	Muslim	Hospital	GBV Center	Counsellor
Ke 5 Post-war	14	14	Not held	Christian	Hospital	GBV Center	Counsellor
KeD 1	36	27	4 years	Muslim	Friend/Trad. med.	Karamoko, Herbalist	Counsellor
KeD 2	40	37	1 night	Christian	Trad. med.	Native treatment, GBV Center	Church, Counsellor
KeD 3	34	33	Not held	Muslim	Herbalist/trad. med.	No	Counsellor Hospital
KeD 4	22	22	Two weeks	Muslim	Friend/trad. med.	No	Counsellor
KeD 5	28	26	Two weeks	Christian	Mother/trad. med.	No	Counsellor
KeD 6	23	10	1 year	Muslim	Father/trad. med.	No	Counsellor
KeD 7	20	15	Nine months	Muslim	No medical attention	Herbalist, Mori-man, Karamoko	Counsellor
KeD 8	25	15	2 years	Muslim	Herbalist/trad. med.	Karamoko	Counsellor
KeD 9	20	12	3 years	Muslim	Grandmother/trad. med.	No	Counsellor and church
KeD 10	20	small	1½ year	Muslim	Herbalist/trad. med.	Karamoko, Mori-man, and others	Counsellor
KeD 11	31	28	1 day	Christian	Herbalist/ trad. med.	No	Counsellor

Notes: 1. WA=Western area; 2. Ma=Makeni town; 3. BD=Bombali district, rural areas; 4. Ko=Koidu town; 5. KD=Kono district rural areas; 6. Ke=Kenema town; 7. KeD=Kenema Districts, rural areas

31

preferred or alternative healing mode. A conversion has taken place in some cases, but in others it seems that they are able to go between the two religions. On the other hand, being a Christian does not mean shutting the traditional society out, as illustrated in the case of a young Christian girl put in a Bundu Society for healing. It is also clear from the table that many try different forms of healing, ranging from herbalists, to the Bundu Society, to Mori-men and Karamokos. Yet only one states that she has consulted a TBA (traditional birth attendant), and no one consulted MCH (maternal child health) aides. When it comes to a preferred healing method, a majority say they prefer counselling. That is hardly surprising since the study was after all carried out with participants in counselling programmes, or skills training programmes that include counselling. Many of the interviewees, however, appear not to have a very clear idea of what counselling entail.

In the table various forms of healing methods at work are presented. As noted in section 3, on limitations of the study, answers are most likely adjusted towards Christian/Western practices partly due to longstanding power hegemonies where Christianity is seen as more advanced than Islam. We should also remember that from colonial days governments have tried to downplay the roles of secret societies and ritual practitioners, as they were long viewed as a threat to a stable state. Such issues have furthered the secrecy of certain practices. Rosalind Shaw locates the roots of this secrecy in socio-cultural changes during the times of the slave raids and later as a tool of resistance in relationship to a dominant state (see Shaw 2000, 2001, 2002). This point is emphasised to highlight that some important issues relating to healing practices could not be accessed for this study.

There are three interrelated forms of healing that must take place after a young person has been sexually abused, namely: medical, psychological and social. As previously outlined, there are various traditional healers inside the Sierra Leone healing complex able to cater for these. Direct medical healing is mainly catered for by herbalists, psychological healing by the Karamoko/Mori-men, and social healing by churches, Soweh mammies and in the ancestor bush, all having their specific roles to play.

6.2. The herbalist

We used native leaves from the bush. We boiled them and put them in a big bowl. I sat down over it so that it healed the sore in my vagina. (20-year-old woman in Kenema District)

One of the rebels caught me and took me to the bush and abused me. He then left me and I tried to get back home. When my grandmother saw me she cried and took me inside for no one to see me. She then went to the bush to find country medicine and then she used it to clean me up. (18-year-old girl in Makeni)

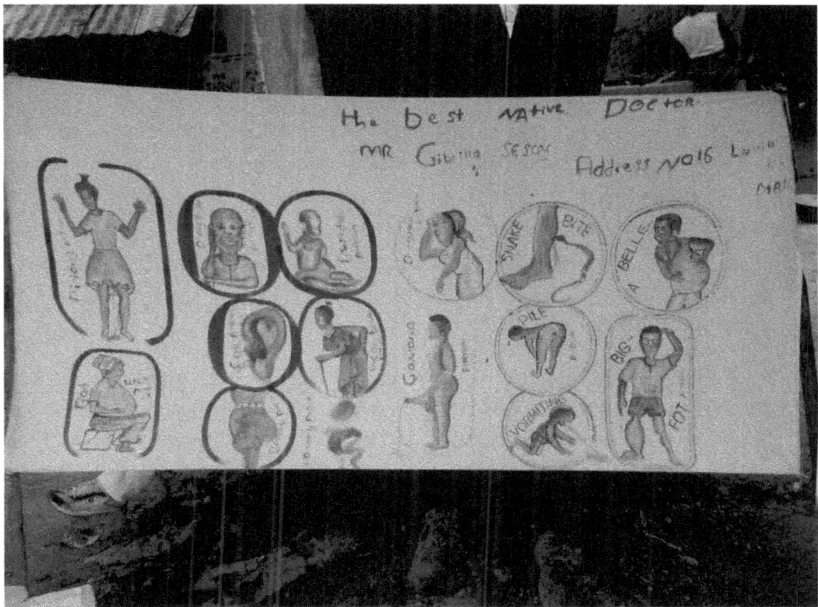

Advertisement for herbal medicine in Makeni.

It is not only specialists in herbs that make use of traditional medicine (local called country medicine, native medicine or bush medicine); as in the above cases it may be a relative who possesses the knowledge. It is, however, important to point out that even specialists in herbs aim to stop direct bleeding but rarely take on more complex issues such as treating people's mental problems. Herbalists seem to hesitate to take on such cases and instead pass them on to the Mori-men. In the above quote it is interesting to note the social stigma attached to sexual abuse, with the girl pointing out the grandmother's strategy of concealing the case from public knowledge by doing the treatment in the house.

In the exploration into the work of herbalists the study found that many herbalists only know how to heal direct wounds. There are even certain herbalists who are exclusively bone-men – who treat broken limbs. This specialization should not be taken too literally since some people publicly known as herbalists also possess knowledge similar to that of the Mori-men. One of those fields is the knowledge of divination. Herbalists and some Mori-men who specialize in this field are sometimes known as "looking grounds" and cater first and foremost for a female clientele. Herbalists seem to be using different techniques for divination, than Mori-men and Karamokos. For instance one herbalist (or "looking ground") in Makeni uses *diegge* (cowries) and in Kenema a herbalist uses his *yorgoi* (pebbles) and *totewei* (stick), while the Mori-men and Karamokos have a preference for "Muslim" methods, including the *Tasabia* (rosary), *Ramla* (numbers), and *Atmera* (writing of verses from the Koran).

Below is an account by a female herbalist of how she cures survivors of sexual abuse. It is interesting to note that she asks both pastors and imams to pray for her clients:

> *I use different kinds of native medicine to cure them. I use two medicines and I use each medicine for a week. I include religious people to help me to pray for the victims, both in the Muslim and Christian way, so that God will help me to cure them. I will also ask the victim to buy a piece of satin, a white fowl, and red and white kola nut and then use it to perform a ceremony. After the ceremony the victim should give the fowl and the red kola nut to a light-skinned man and the white kola to a woman. I can also cure the abuser by splashing them with country medicine and giving them herbs to drink in order to clean their stomach.* (Herbalist in Freetown)

A herbalist in Makeni makes a comparison with modern Western medicine. In this case he is ready to try to work on cases handling mental problems, which also implies ridding clients of evil spirits.

I can cure the bleeding of a raped person. You can try it either our way or the English way. Some try it in a different way but later come here. I give them medicine to drink and rice flour… There is also a medicine for people with mental problems. They drink it and then you make rope (Sebe) with it. To make the heart go cold (leave psychological problems behind) there is also a medicine. (Herbalist in Makeni)

Items in the room of a herbalist in Makeni.

A girl in Bombali District recounted that she was taken to a TBA to be treated after being sexually abused. The TBA cured her with herbs and made a Sebe (country rope and herb medicine) for her to put around her waist. In this case the TBA was using the healing techniques of the herbalist and the Mori-man/Karamoko.

6.3. The Karamoko and the Mori-man

I was frustrated – I nearly went off (went mad). But then my mother took me to the Mori-man who gave me lasmami to drink. (20-year-old woman in a Kenema village)

I was treated by the Mori-man. He boiled medicines and "smoked" us with it (putting the head over a pot with boiled leaves to let the person inhale the steam). The water contained leaves, country sapo (twinned rattan, commonly used for scrubbing the body when taking a bath), and black soap. He then chanted and threw ashes on us and finally he asked us to shower in the water. (16-year-old girl from Freetown).

The Karamoko will help me to come out of my experiences by writing Arabic and put it inside a bottle and then giving it to me to drink from. Then he will rub bitter medicine on my body whenever I want to go out. The Mori-man will help you to look good among your friends, and even for me to get a good husband. He will ask me to

35

buy kola nuts, incense and black, white and red cloth and perform a ritual so I will stop thinking about what happened. (21-year-old woman in Koidu)

The herbalist boiled native herbs and put it in a bowl and asked me to sit on it so that the medicine would cleanse me. Then he asked me to bring clothes (white, red and black), then he asked me to put them on. (21-year-old woman in Koidu)

From the above accounts we get some ideas of the healing ceremonies that Mori-men and Karamokos can carry out to aid young survivors of sexual abuse. From the research it seems quite clear that they play a central role in the individual psychological healing of young people who have been sexually abused. For instance a Soweh mammy in Makeni was asked about mental illness, and stated that it is the Mori-men and Karamokos that take care of people who are mentally ill: *"I can't treat spirits, but only Mori-men can cure that"*. Likewise a female herbalist in Freetown said that if she comes across a grave case of mental distress she will take the person to consult a Mori-man in nearby Lungi. Whilst some Mori-men avoid exposing their work to outsiders, others appear quite open:

> *I cured 17 women for that during the war, but they are fewer now.* (Mori-man in Makeni)

In this research people do not make any real distinction between Mori-men and Karamokos; if anything, the Karamoko is more of a Muslim teacher with young followers and the Mori-man is specialized in "Muslim" medicine and divination. There are several other names that cover this category, including Alpha, Kaamo,[1] and at times "looking ground" – even if this last set of diviners might fit within the herbalist category. At the other end of the spectrum we also find imams carrying out work of the Mori-men, like this imam in Kono District:

> *My own two daughters were abducted during the war. One looked good when she came home, the other was pale. I went to the bush myself to find herbs, and then I washed them and prayed for them.* (Senior imam in Kono District)

Mori-men will generally first consult God in order to find out if they have the power to heal the client who has come to consult them. They use various techniques for this, like the *Tasabia* (rosary), *Ramla* (numbers) and *Atmera*

---

1. A common term in Mende.

(writing verses from the Koran). These are the most Muslim of the practices, but other semi-Muslim diviners like "looking grounds" use other techniques. When it comes to the result of the divination, if the session comes up with a positive result the Mori-man will take on the task of curing the survivor. If not he might be able to recommend the case to a senior Mori-man.

I sometimes take it to my senior if the case is serious (Karamoko, Freetown).

There are two main techniques used for the treatment of young sexually abused survivors. The first and most direct one is the *Zaraba,* the "holy washing". An imam in Koidu makes the distinction between *holy washing* (for those who have gone mad) and *holy cleansing* (for those who want money and to become leaders).

The Alpha (Mori-man or Karamoko) will wash the person in a big basin with warm water and native soap. She will be covered by a piece of cloth and then I will read over her. I will prepare nasi (holy water, also called lasmami) for her. Sometimes I will be indoors for seven days for prayer. I will only eat rice flower and honey. I will sleep on the floor and pray for the victim. The victim will be in the same house and will eat and rest. (Imam in Koidu)

The other ceremony is the *Sara.* Often people would say that they "pull *Sara*" – that is, make a sacrifice, for instance of chicken, rice, other food items and even clothes. There are specific *Sara* clothes that may accompany the ceremony.

The *Sara* is a sacrifice in order to get something in return. In the case of sexually abused people it is a way to get rid of spirits that are not allowing the survivor to rest. The function is thus similar to the *Zaraba* (holy washing).

In this sense the practitioners are making a distinction between bodily, or medical, healing and psychological healing. As suggested above, mental sickness is viewed as being caused by something external to the body and indeed the psychological healing practices of the Mori-men and Karamokos are concerned with re-externalizing the evil spirit that is causing the mental trauma. An art of the Mori-men is to be able to detect *djinas* (evil spirits) and they will use various divination techniques (*Tasabia, Ramla and Atmera*) to locate it:

In some cases the person will not even talk when they come to me, but through the looking ground I will see that there is a djina there. (Mori-man in Makeni)

Sara clothes for sale in Ngo town.

carry out such a task, or they may say as a matter of course that such patients should go to other Mori-men and healers. One of the Makeni-based Mori-men stated that if a case is grave he might recommend them to go to the hospital because he is *"afraid of government if something bad will happen"*. In reality it is likely that Mori-men are more afraid of an angry mob of relatives than the government, but it is worthwhile pointing out that both security and reputation is at risk if patients die during treatment. Naturally, not all the medicine that the Mori-men make is used for healing purposes; some is used for causing problems:

> *I will make Sebe for the heart to go cold and to put fire between two people.* (Mori-man in Makeni)

Due to this duality in their practice there are constant rumors of Mori-men being involved in cases of witchcraft.

Some (for example a Mori-man in Makeni) state that they can also perform communal cleansing sacrifices, but their role is unclear. Mori-men are generally more involved in individual healing, but when it comes to family matters they are also influential:

> *We try to encourage the family not to give her problems when she is healing. I have a medicine for making the family re-accept a girl who has been sexually abused.* (Mori-man in Kenema)

However, not all patients are satisfied with the final outcome of the healing rituals:

> *I went to a Karamoko once. He told me to buy some items to perform a ritual. I bought kola nuts, a fowl, rice, pepper and salt. But it was all in vain because he could not cure my stomach or help me with my trauma.* (25-year-old woman in a Kenema village)

It is also sometimes rumored that Karamokos and Mori-men take sexual advantage of their positions. There is, however, little indicating that they would be more inclined to such behavior than other men with socio-economic power.

6.4. The Soweh mammy and female herbalist (*Kuntumoi musu*)[1]

> *The Diba treated me with herbs from the bush. She heated herbs over the fire and applied it on the wounds in my vagina. I prayed in water and then my "heart go cold".* (27-year-old woman in Kono District)

> *My mother took me to the Bundu Society. There I was initiated and they also treated me with different types of herbs.* (16-year-old girl in Kono District)

As we see in these short accounts, the way the Soweh mammies use medicine does not seem too dissimilar from the other healers within the traditional healing complex. It is, however, far from clear what they are really doing. What help, other than purely medical, do sexually abused women get from the Sowehs?

> *The Diba (Soweh mammy) will help me in so many different ways, but that will happen inside the Bundu bush so I can't explain it to you in detail.* (21-year-old woman in Koidu)

Some of their practices are wrapped in secrecy; however, part of the knowledge of these Soweh mammies is known to be outside the secrecy of the Bundu bush and in this function they work in many ways like the herbalists. This section will give prominence to the Soweh mammies' own accounts.

---

1. In the Kono language.

Yes, I do help them. I perform different types of ceremonies to help them make their hearts cold. I mostly use country medicine to perform these ceremonies. (Soweh Mammy, Freetown).

I do not believe in religion (i.e. Islam or Christianity). I go through spirits and these spirits will guide me to what kind of medicine I will use. (Soweh Mammy, Freetown)

In making sacrifices Sowehs use items very similar to the other healers discussed above:

The person will be asked to cleanse the bush: provide a goat, a fowl, 5 gallons of palm oil, rice and money to provide sacrifice for the gods. For the ritual I use a lappa, a goat, fanganama (Krio word – mixture of food),[1] country fish, and a red fowl. (Soweh mammy, Makeni)

It is the same ritual that is done for cleansing a woman who has lost her husband. The only thing is that the leaves are different. They are taken to the stream with the prepared herbs, black soap, a hen of any color, and some rice for the hen to eat. The rice will be used for interpretation by the herbalist. That is if the hen eats the rice for the sexually abused woman then she is finally cleansed of the bad luck. (Soweh mammy in Kono District)

It is interesting to note that whilst the Soweh mammy from Freetown quoted above states that she does not believe in religion, the next two Sowehs say that religion is important. The first states that she is a Christian herself, while the second states that she makes use of both Christian and Muslim prayers by going to both the pastor and Mori-man.

I have successfully treated 30 young women who have been sexually abused. I will go to the bush and collect many different herbs; I will boil them and then make the patient sit in a big bowl. I will also pray, because I am a Christian. (Soweh mammy in Kono District)

I will ask them to buy palm oil, kola nuts, a fowl, salt and sugar. Sometimes I will provide them myself as the victims cannot afford them. I will then take them to the river and wash them. I will ask them not to have sex with men for three months because if they do so they will not be cured. Religion is very important. I will call God to direct me and I will pray in water and also take the victim to the pastor in the village to pray for them. I will also take them to the Mori-man to give them medicine for their "heart to go cold" (Soweh mammy in Bombali District)

1. In Mende, *Fangani.*

Other Soweh mammies' statements make clear that psychological healing is not part of their ordinary work.

> *If they "go off" (go mad, I will take them to the Karamoko to treat them with Arabic water (lasmami).* (Soweh mammy in Bombali District)

> *The Karamoko and the Mori-man treat mentally ill people. I can only pray for them.* (Soweh mammy in Koidu town)

Our material on Soweh mammies and the Bundu bush is insufficient for drawing direct conclusions. However we can conclude that the Bundu Society and their Sowehs are involved in social cleansing ceremonies. Knowledge about Soweh mammies' important social and political roles in wider society and the fact that Bundu is a leading sustaining factor in the female moral world further account for their importance in the Sierra Leone healing complex.

6.5. Cleansing the bush

> *We take the perpetrators to the police, but we are also asking the perpetrators to clean the bush by bringing a goat, palm oil, rice, a fowl and kola nuts to perform a ritual to the gods. Later he will go to jail.* (Soweh mammy in Kenema District)

Cleansing the bush is a quite open expression, where bush can refer to Bundu or Poro (the male secret society), but also to sacrifice to honor the ancestral bush. Cleansing the bush refers to a communal activity, not an individual one. When questions concerning social cleansings were asked, very disparate answers were given. In a number of instances the response was to deny the existence of this type of ceremony.

> *Here we don't have any cleansing ceremonies (for victims of sexual abuse) but they have that in Tanzania.* (Young man in Bombali District)

In Western Area and Bombali District, few traces of cleansing ceremonies were discovered. According to NGO staff in Makeni, though not backed up in other accounts, there are special cleansing activities within the Bundu Society. In Kenema District a chief suggested that in the past there were ancestral offerings in Kenema town itself:

We used to have ceremonies down by the river to satisfy our ancestors. This was a long time ago and I do not think it is possible to recreate it. (Chief in Kenema)

A Mori-man invited the research team to participate in such a ceremony in December 2004:

April last year we had a ceremony back in my village for the people who died in the war. We are planning another one in December. Back in the villages, people do ceremonies for separated villagers to return. It is made to show unity and shows relatives that whatever they have done they are forgiven. (Mori-man in Kenema)

It is, however, far from clear whether this is part of a bush-cleansing tradition or something else. There is insufficient material of hand to make any suggestions on this matter. The most interesting case of bush-cleansings appears to be Kono District where several accounts of this practice were encountered. In several Kono villages people talked about ceremonies to please the ancestors.

After getting medicine from the herbalist (to stop the bleeding etc.) my husband made an overall ritual to our ancestors. My husband is a chief and it is a curse if such a thing (sexual abuse) happens to a chief's wife. The herbalist asked us to buy a goat, black, white and red cloth, rice and palm oil for the ritual. He performed the ceremony and cooked plenty food and gave it to the villagers. Then he gave me the ritual dress to put it on every day underneath my dress. (Chief's wife in Kono District)

The person responsible for this ceremony is the *Kongoe Ya Sue*. According to an interviewee the meaning of these Kono words is "the one that stands before the hill", where the hill is the symbolic dwelling of the ancestors. There are two *Kongoe Ya Sue*, one for women and one for men. The *Kongoe Ya Sue* is the "ancestral representative" in society, or the intermediary between the society and the ancestors. It is the *Kongoe Ya Sue* who is responsible for keeping the ancestors content and the one who should get their permission for reaccepting ex-combatants and young abducted women alike. In three different locations in rural Kono District a record of this type of cleansing ceremony involving the entire community was taken. In one village people stated that it is also done in advance to let the ancestors invite the lost boys and girls of the community to come home. One of the secular functions of the ceremony is that once the ancestral acceptance of the young girls is given social acceptance follows. In one place the interviewee stated that due to this ceremony girls and young women would not face any problems in returning to their families or husbands and there would be no future marriage problems. All the people, including pastors and imams, take part in the ceremony, as they are all asked to pray.

6.6. The pastor

The only medicine is prayer. (17-year-old girl in Makeni)

The church offers special prayers for me to forget about my trauma. (20-year-old woman in Kenema District)

As we have seen in the interviews with sexually abused young women many consider the churches a good place to be healed. With a focus on the individual the pastor is often able to do an effective healing job. A pastor in a Born-Again church gives an example of how young girls who come to the church look:

> *You can often not see anything on them. But they might appear depressed, downcast, closed, poor and pale. They feel rejected by society. A few of them go crazy – a result of abusive drinking and use of drugs. They are often rebellious and have a hard time to believe that God is there. People fear the girls who have been with rebels. There is no trust and they are often transmitters of diseases. But we help them with counselling, telling them that God cares for them.* (Pastor in Koidu)

It is also interesting to see how the pastor views churches as avenues to reacceptance in broader society.[1]

> *Born-Again churches work as shelters for these young girls, even for rebel soldiers, because "God don change am". Born-Again churches is a guarantee. Look at Charles Taylor's number 1 bodyguard; he is now a Born-Again pastor.[2] In this way sexually abused women find it convenient to become Born-Again.* (Pastor in Koidu)

Churches offer little more than prayer as their method of healing the wounds of war, yet it should be stated that exorcisms of demons and devils are very much in line with the functions of the other healing practices inside the traditional healing complex, and this further highlights the concept of external

1. Churches are also important for the reintegration of ex-combatant soldiers, as I have written about elsewhere (Utas 2005c).
2. The reference is to former Liberian president and rebel leader Charles Taylor. It is a fact that many of the earlier warlords, including Taylor himself, and high-ranking commanders have become Born-Again Christians in the aftermath of the civil war. The most well-known is General 'Butt-Naked' who is now a well-known pastor.

mental illness, with the therapeutic edge being the re-externalizing of spirits inhabiting the individual. Survivors of sexual abuse in Sierra Leone thus have the possibility of moving between healing practices within the healing complex without leaving behind the basic psycho-social model of mental illness as external to the body. In this vein it is interesting to view the many converts from Islam to Christianity among the interviewees.

Many young sexually abused women came to our church during the war. Most of them were Muslims but they converted to Christianity. In fact many convert to Christianity because they do not have the means to pay consultation fees to herbalists and Mori-men. (Pastor in Kenema)

After all, the cosmology remains the same.

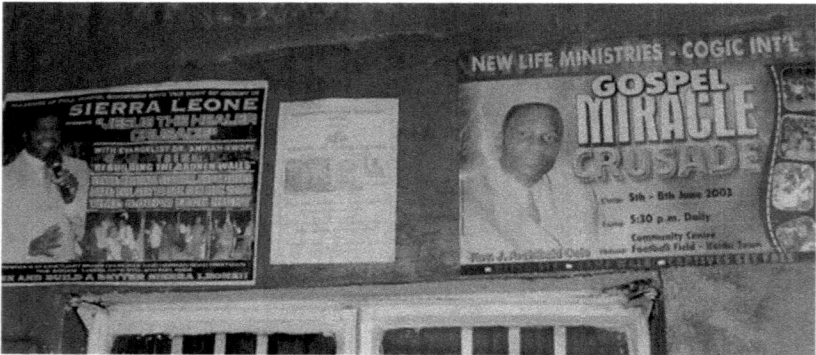

Front door of church in Koidu.

6.7. Talking trauma – notes on counselling

I want to ask whether trauma counsellors are coming to create job facilities for us. (20-year-old woman from Makeni)

Although the activities within the trauma counselling projects propelled by the international community are not a main component of this study it is still interesting to see how this newcomer is coping in relation to the Sierra Leone healing complex. In many cases young survivors of sexual abuse state that they would like to receive more individual attention from counsellors. But who are the counsellors and what are they doing, and what kind of attention do the survivors have in mind? Western-modeled trauma counselling can be viewed as the most recent contribution to the Sierra Leone healing complex and it is almost entirely driven by the Western aid community. Psycho-social counselling components are commonplace in many emergency aid programmes, ranging from group exercises to efforts to assist traumatized individuals. In most cases counsellors' knowledge of Western psychology is scant and most have learnt the "trade" in *training of trainers* workshops. In some cases counsellors are both talented and devoted, but there are rarely sufficient resources available to make any real input. It is clear from the answers in this study that many beneficiaries do not have a clear idea what a counsellor should do, as this quote suggests:

> *A trauma counsellor can open a center for young victims to learned skilled trades.* (20-year-old woman from Koidu)

At the same time many state that real benefits are few, like this young woman from Makeni:

> *Counsellors will only ask you plenty questions. Then they will promise that they will help you with the medical job, but at the end of the day nothing will come out of it.* (18-year-old girl from Makeni)

It also appears that the psycho-social counselling is not seen as important; rather it is the prospect of getting education that counts for most participants. Like this girl:

> *I would like to talk to a trauma counsellor of the NGOs because I believe that they will assist people to come out of it by creating job facilities and skilled training programmes.* (17-year-old girl from Makeni)

Counselling appears to be a vague concept in the minds of survivors of sexual abuse. In many cases counselling is confused with skills training programmes. To make stand-alone Western trauma counselling work to a satisfactory degree would demand massive investments in knowledge and resources, and furthermore it would take many years to build up sufficient structures. If the international community has the best intentions towards survivors of sexual abuse in the post-conflict setting it is necessary instead to "localize" projects, become involved with the healing complex and learn from the traditional players. After all "external" actors belonging to Islam and Christianity were successful exactly because they incorporated local traditions. Today they are the main actors.

7. Findings and recommendations

7.1. Social approaches towards the sexually abused

Girls and young women who have been abused are treated in widely differing ways. The study points towards this complexity rather than in one direction.

1. There is a certain social stigma that goes with having been sexually abused.

2. Families of sexual abuse survivors often try to hide the occurrence and it is quite often not talked about in their homes. On the other hand, few of the young women who have returned to family homes appear to be maltreated. Often survivors say that they are most open about their trauma with elderly relatives.

3. Some sexual abuse survivors report that friends insult them. On the other hand many survivors state that they are able to talk to their friends about their trauma, especially if they have gone through the same experiences.

4. Survivors state that it is difficult to get married if you have been sexually abused; yet others state that after the experience of abuse they have no wish to have intimate relationships with men.

5. A few survivors state that they are back with their husbands and there are cases in the interview material that show how husbands are the ones who initially aid their wives in the immediate post-abuse phase.

6. Many girls and young women who became pregnant as a result of sexual abuse during the war indicated that some friends and neighbours insult and label their children by calling them "rebel pikins" or something similar.

7. Many respondents indicated that sexual abuse in the non-war setting might lead to marriage between survivor and perpetrator. The respond-

ents indicated that several cases of sexual abuse are still settled between the survivor's and perpetrator's families, involving damage payment.

8. There are several techniques used to improve a woman's prospects:

9. It appears that the sheer number of young women who were sexually abused during the war years (the Physicians for Human Rights report estimated the number to be between 50,000 and 64,000 among the IDP population alone) made it easier for survivors to talk to other people about their experience and thereby reduce the level of trauma. The war context may have shielded the survivor from some of the social stigmatization.

10. The intensive peace and reconciliation education carried out by government, (I)NGOs and community-based organizations (CBOs) also made it easier for survivors and community members to talk about sexual abuse. This community awareness may be directly related to the increased reporting of sexual abuse to the police.

11. Education and skills training programmes are yet other avenues of establishing an independent self in relation to local society. New skills may redirect the minds of people in the community.

12. Traditional healing and cleansing activities for survivors of sexual abuse during the war appear to be an important process for their being reaccepted and reintegrated in local communities.

7.2. Girls' and young women's practices related to traditional healing

The 50 interviews conducted with girls and young women who were sexually abused during or after the civil war found that:

1. A majority, as many as 83%, of those who were sexual abused during the war, were initially treated with traditional medicine (herbs and leaves) shortly after the assault.

2. Generally the initial traditional medicine consultation resulted in a herbal treatment for physical injuries, but this treatment also opened up the opportunity for other traditional healing practices to be used.

3. Fewer survivors (34% of respondents to the question) reported the continued use of traditional methods and most stated that the church or counselling were preferred avenues for psychological healing.

4. No direct links were found between religion and a particular form (physical, social, spiritual or psychological) of treatment. Even though many of the traditional healing methods (including the services of Karamokos and Mori-men) include practices that have their roots in Islam, the study could not link young Muslim survivors with these treatments.

5. The study found that many young Muslim survivors turned to the Christian Church services in their quest for healing.

6. The study revealed that young people who have been sexually abused try many different methods to get well. In fact it is likely that young survivors of sexual abuse go through several, if not all, different traditional healing methods (Christian, herbalist, Mori-men) in their search for one that works.

7.3. Findings on traditional healers

1. The Sierra Leone healing complex consists of a number of interlinked practices by traditional healing practitioners (e.g. Karamokos, Morimen, Sowehs, and pastors). These practices have been shaped and reshaped by historical processes. Those of Christian or Muslim origin have adapted to a local culture but simultaneously they have also reshaped local culture.

2. In Sierra Leone it is not meaningful to talk about traditional healing practices if Christianity and Islam are not included.

3. Mental illness is viewed as an external entity in Sierra Leonean culture. It is conceived of as attacks by spirits, bush devils or demons. All healing practices, including those of the Christian church, are involved in re-

externalizing such spirits. The mental healing of sexual abuse survivors also follows this logic.

4. There are three forms of interrelated healing that must take place after a young person has been sexually abused, namely (1) medical, or physical, (2) psychological and (3) social. All to some extent include spiritual healing.

The study found that the Sierra Leonean traditional healing complex is able to cater for: (1) direct medical, or physical, healing, mainly through the herbalists; (2) psychological healing through the Karamokos/Mori-men; and (3) social healing through the churches, Soweh mammies, and in the ancestor bush. The "healing players" all have specific roles to play:

1. The herbalists are mainly involved with medical healing and more importantly active providers of herbs.

2. With direct roots in Islamic divination and healing rituals, the practices of Karamokos and Mori-men are central to the psychological healing of many young survivors. Twenty per cent of survivor accounts documented mention encounters with Karamokos and Mori-men. It is believed that there has been a certain underreporting by survivors on the use of traditional healers as they may have thought that only NGO or Christian Church service providers should be mentioned due to previous involvement with NGOs and an understanding that traditional healing should be "secret". Most of the survivors in this study were referred by NGOs who implicitly encourage people to present themselves as being "urban" and "Christian". Judging from interviews with local leaders as well as Karmokos' and Mori-men's own accounts their work is of major importance in the psychological healing of survivors of sexual abuse.

3. The Soweh mammies are the leaders of the Bundu Society. Initiates of this Society will have access to healing activities inside the Bundu Society, yet because of the secrecy of this society it is very difficult to know what actually transpires.[1] The research indicates that Soweh mammies often have healing roles outside the Bundu Society that resemble those of the herbalists. It also appears that inside the Bundu

1. As Dellenborg has shown, the socialization aspects of the secret society are more important than the content of it (2007: 24). In that way healing within Bundu society is a psycho-social reintegration or resocialization process.

Society certain cleansing rituals are performed for the re-acceptance of abducted girls and young women in the larger society. Finally we must acknowledge that despite our lack of knowledge of what happens inside the Bundu Society if survivors of sexual abuse are of the opinion that activities there are important for their healing then such endeavors should be encouraged.

4. The Bundu societies are not the only providers of social cleansing rituals; as found in Kono District, it appears that in some villages the entire community is involved in social cleansing rituals for the reunified male and female child ex-combatants and returning "bush" wives. In these cases it involves the ancestral bush and the elder, *the Kongoe Ya Sue,* responsible for that shrine, and the ritual is performed to cleanse individuals as well as the entire society.

5. Christian churches also play important roles in healing survivors of sexual abuse. Born-Again evangelical churches are instrumental in both mental and social healing of sexual abuse survivors. From the interviews it is clear that many young Muslim survivors have converted to Christianity. A pastor in one church pointed out that the church's psychosocial healing is free of charge, whilst herbalists and Karamokos/Morimen demand high fees.[1]

7.4. Recommendations

• NGOs and government service delivery systems working with survivors of sexual abuse should utilize appropriate and safe traditional healing methods in an advantageous way, instead of forcing change or creating separate structures. This study argues that the traditional healing complex in Sierra Leone is in a constant process of reshaping and reformulation. Historical processes have always brought about change in such an innovative and flexible system, as for instance Rosalind Shaw has pointed out in her book *Memories of the Slave Trade* (2002). The direct outcomes of the Sierra Leonean civil war, as well as the considerable impact of (I)NGO service delivery in post-war Sierra Leone,

---

1. On the other hand churches expect high voluntary contributions from their congregations.

both contribute towards change in the country's fragmented historical processes. Change in the "traditional healing complex" is an ongoing process to which (I)NGO service delivery directly contributes.

• It is crucial to work with the various actors within the traditional healing complex. It is possible to contribute and maintain the traditional healing complex in Sierra Leone, and at the same time, work for change, for instance. From a Western perspective the prevalence of female genital mutilation (FGM) in the Bundu bush is harmful to young female children. However, if a process-oriented approach to society is taken, then interacting with the local healing complex will involve observations, dialogue and analysis within the cultural process, and indirect influence will bring about positive change within the local healing complex itself.

• The provision of support for establishing traditional medical centers (TMCs) is recommended. Today many traditional healers complain about the squalid conditions under which they practice their vocations. At times herbalists do not have access to new razor blades, although they know that HIV may be spread through the use of contaminated razor blades. At times the practitioners will find it difficult to host their patients for the required time, due to lack of space in their homes. The practitioners interviewed supported the idea of establishing TMCs. A TMC would be a place where traditional practitioners could continue to practice their trades, extend their cooperation, establish safe and lawful traditional healing procedures, and also have access to hygienic places and equipment. It would allow the donor better control over practices, enabling them to gain easier entry into what the practitioners are doing, and also to advocate change from the inside. FGM could be addressed in these TMCs. If young people who have been sexually abused cannot afford the healings services at the TMCs then *pro bono* access could be provided in exchange for free rental space for the practitioners at a TMC.

• A positive way to contribute to individual and social healing in local communities would be to contribute to the "social cleansings" *(Kongoe ya sue* in Kono) that are currently taking place. From the study it appears that these social cleansing ceremonies occur most frequently in Kono

District. The ceremonies aim at asking the forefathers for forgiveness and acceptance within the community of the young community members who have returned to the community even if they have committed severe crimes (murder, rape) during the war. These ceremonies also appear to be a socially positive force for a child who has been sexually abused, her family and the community. The Bundu Society also has similar types of ceremonies for members, although the study was not able to gain enough information about these practices.

- Referring sexual abuse survivors to external service providers, such as NGOs, may have long-term negative effects on the survivors' social re-integration. Participating in NGO projects for survivors of sexual abuse may be a risk for girls and young women if their secrets become public. Furthermore, when these projects are terminated or downscaled, and the economic and social support of these individuals disappears, there is a risk that they will experience re-stigmatization.

- Collaboration between and integration of NGO and traditional service providers for sexually abused survivors must take place soon after a conflict, so that sustainable community mechanisms can be put on place.

- More targeted research is needed to increase knowledge on matters concerning traditional healing. This study only begins to identify the issues surrounding sexual abuse and traditional healing. The secrecy within the traditional healing complex, especially in the Bundu Society, greatly inhibited this study's findings. A more thorough understanding of social cleansing ceremonies would also enable us to find instances where aid would be appropriate.

Appendices

A. Acknowledgements

This work would not have been carried out in such a stringent manner if it had not been for my two hardworking assistants: Umu Utas, who carried out most of the interviews in Freetown, as well as taking care of our two children, and Mabinti Bangura who conducted the interviews with girls and young women in the Sierra Leone interior. The third person I wish to thank is our driver Mr. Sidique who brought us safely and punctually to all locations. At UNICEF I would especially like to thank Donald Robertshaw and his staff at the Child Protection Unit. The NGOs that helped us greatly are Coopi, IRC, AFC, Caritas Makeni and CCSL. In Sweden I wish to thank Chris Coulter for sharing her knowledge on young women in war torn Sierra Leone and Liselott Dellenborg for her thorough and well-informed review.

B. List of abbreviations

CBO	Community Based Organisation
CPU	Child Protection Unit
CRC UN	Convention on the Rights of the Child
FGM	Female Genital Mutilation
GBV	Gender Based Violence
IDP	Internally Displaced Person
INGO	International Non-Government Organisation
MCH Aides	Mother Children Health Aides
RUF	Revolutionary United Front
TBA	Traditional Birth Attendant
TMC	Traditional Medical Center

C. Literature

Argenti-Pillen, Alex. 2003. *Masking Terror: How women contain violence in Southern Sri Lanka*. Philadelphia. University of Pennsylvania Press.

Bellman, Beryl. 1984. *The Language of secrecy: symbols & metaphors in Poro ritual*. New Brunswick: Rutgers University Press.

Coulter, Chris. 2006. *Being a bush wife: women's lives through war and peace in Northern Sierra Leone*. Dissertation: Uppsala University.

Dellenborg, Liselott. 2007. *Multiple meanings of female initiations: "circumcision" among Jola women in Lower Casamance, Senegal*. Dissertation: Gothenburg University.

Ferme, Mariane. C. 2001. *The underneath of things: violence, history, and the everyday in Sierra Leone*. Berkeley: University of California Press.

Gberie, Lansana. 2003. *A dirty war in Sierra Leone: the RUF and the destruction of Sierra Leone*. London: Hurst.

Honwana, Alcinda. 1997. Healing for peace: traditional healers and post-war reconstruction in Southern Mozambique. In *Peace and conflict: journal of peace psychology* 3:293-305.

___1999. The collective body: challenging western concepts of trauma and healing. In *Track Two* (July 1999):30-35)

___2001. Children of war: understanding war and war cleansing in Mozambique and Angola. In *Civilians in war*. Ed. Simon Chesterman. Boulder: Lynne Reinner.

Kaplan, Suzanne. 2005. *Children in Africa with experiences of massive trauma*. Stockholm: Sida Department for Research Cooperation.

Keen, David. 2005. *Conflict and Collusion in Sierra Leone*. Oxford: James Currey.

Metcalf, Peter. 2002. *They lie, we lie: getting on with anthropology*. London: Routledge.

Nordstrom Carolyn. 1997a. *A different kind of war story*. Philadelphia: University of Pennsylvania Press.

___1997b. *Girls and warzones: troubling questions*. Uppsala: Life & Peace Institute.

Persson, Mariam. 2005. *"In their eyes we'll always be rebels" – A minor field study of female ex-combatants in Sierra Leone*, Minor field study series 50 (Development Studies) Uppsala University.

Physicians for Human Rights 2002. *War-related sexual violence in Sierra Leone*.

Richards, Paul. 1996. *Fighting for the rain forest: war, youth and resources in Sierra Leone*. Oxford: James Currey.

Robertshaw, Donald. 2004. Historical context of DDR and Girls left behind project. Oral presentation at the *Technical meeting on The girls left behind and traditional healing methods for sexual abuse victims*. Bintumani Hotel, Freetown, August 24-26, 2004.

Shaw, Rosalind. 2000. "Tok af, lef af": a political economy of Temne techniques of secrecy and self. In *African philosophy as cultural inquiry*. Eds. Ivan Karp & D.A. Masolo.

____2001. Cannibal transformations: colonialism and commodification in the Sierra Leone hinterland. In *Magical interpretations, material realities: modernity, witchcraft and the occult in post-colonial Africa*. Eds. Henrietta Moore & Todd Sanders. London: Routledge.

____2002. *Memories of the slave trade: ritual and the historical imagination in Sierra Leone*. Chicago: University of Chicago Press.

Utas, Mats. 2003. *Sweet Battlefields: Youth and the Liberian Civil War*. PhD Thesis, Department of Cultural Anthropology, Uppsala University Dissertations in Cultural Anthropology, 2003.

____2005a. Agency of Victims: young women's survival strategies in the Liberian Civil War. In *Makers and Breakers; Made and Broken: Children and Youth as Emerging Categories in Postcolonial Africa*. Eds. Filip de Boeck & Alcinda Honwana. Oxford: James Currey.

____2005b. "Victimcy, Girlfriending, Soldiering: Tactic Agency in a Young Woman's Social Navigation of the Liberian War Zone." *Anthropological Quarterly* 78, no. 2 (2005):403-430.

____2005c. Building a future? The reintegration and re-marginalisation of young ex-combatants in Liberia. In *No Peace, No War: Living Beyond Conflict*. Ed. Paul Richards, Oxford: James Currey.